DO NOT REMOVE CARDS FROM THIS POCKET
A CHARGE OF 10¢ WILL BE MADE FOR A
MISSING CARD

AV 042568

DATE DUE	DATE DUE
OCT 23 1980	

THE CHICAGO PUBLIC LIBRARY

AVALON BRANCH
8802 S. STONY ISLAND AVE.
CHICAGO, ILLINOIS 60617

FORM 19

ARTHUR ZAIDENBERG

How
to Draw the
WILD WEST

ABELARD-SCHUMAN NEW YORK · LONDON
An Intext Publisher

BOOKS BY ARTHUR ZAIDENBERG

Library of Congress Cataloging in Publication Data

Zaidenberg, Arthur, 1903-
    How to draw the Wild West.

    SUMMARY: Step-by-step instructions for the beginning artist in drawing cowboys, Indians, stage coaches, covered wagons, and other Western scenes.
    1. The West—Description and travel—Views. 2. Drawing—Instruction—Juvenile literature. [1. The West—Description and travel. 2. Drawing—Instruction] I. Title.
NC655.Z32   741.2   71-156848
ISBN 0-200-71846-O
ISBN 0-200-71847-9   Reinforced Edition

Second Impression, 1973
Published on the same day in Canada by Longman Canada Limited.
First Published in Great Britain in 1973
Designed by The Etheredges

NEW YORK
Abelard-Schuman
Limited
257 Park Avenue So
10010

LONDON
Abelard-Schuman
Limited
450 Edgware Road W2 1EG
and
24 Market Square Aylesbury

Printed in the United States of America

Contents

Introduction

Learning to draw, if you plan to be a serious artist, is a long process. Drawing well requires your complete devotion and a great deal of time. However, there are many thousands of people who have learned to draw pictures, pleasing to both themselves and their friends.

When you were very young you probably drew pictures of things about you, and from your imagination. However, most of us lose this ability to express ourselves when we reach the age of ten or twelve. Except for the few who have "talent," we give up drawing for pleasure.

You have obviously retained your interest in drawing or you would not have opened this book. It is my firm belief that if you have an interest in drawing, you can learn to draw.

You have more dexterity now than when you were quite young. That is demonstrated by the fact that you can write script. The ability to write in clear, flowing script calls for the same skill required to draw a figure or an animal.

Add to that dexterity your imagination, developed through reading and observing, and you may be sure that, with reasonable practice, you will soon be able to draw almost anything you wish.

The Wild West is a subject which excites the imagination of everyone. It has been of special interest to artists.

In this book I have picked many familiar characters and scenes of the West and drawn them in simple, direct terms. In many cases the steps in drawing them are demonstrated.

Do not merely copy my drawings. Try to follow the steps shown in constructing proportions.. Apply what you learn from my drawings to your own drawings, adding your own view point and emotions. Remember to express *yourself* as an artist.

Draw the figures first in the simple or rough sketch positions demonstrated throughout this book. When you have learned to construct them in proportion, then draw your own figures in a wider variety of actions. Add clothes and decorations using this and other books about the West as a source of research.

Drawing Materials

The drawings in this book were made with either carbon pencil or pen and India ink.

Here is a list of materials you should have in order to make drawings in a similar manner. All the materials mentioned are available in most stationery stores and all artist supply shops.

For your pencil drawings buy at least three carbon pencils varying from soft to medium hard, labeled 3B, B and HB.

You will need a soap eraser, which is soft and crumbly, and a kneaded rubber eraser to keep your pencil drawings clean, However, do not rely too much on your eraser. Think instead about what you want to draw first, then draw it carefully. Always sketch very lightly at first and you will find that you almost don't need an eraser.

Buy a good pencil sharpener or a sandpaper pad so that your pencil points will always be sharp. A dull point makes a dull drawing.

For drawing with ink, buy a pen with several points and a bottle of India ink. India ink is a special drawing ink and gives a rich black and waterproof line. You may also use an ordinary writing pen but you will find that an artist's pen gives you much better results.

Get at least two sketch pads, one about 9″ x 12″ and the other small enough to fit in your pocket. There are many varieties of drawing paper and you will soon discover the type of paper that suits you best.

Remember that the sketch pad habit will speed you on your way to skillful drawing. Sketch everything of interest around you and you will soon become proficient. When you cannot sketch, observe and then sketch from memory when you can.

Indians

The early West was peopled by a variety of tribes of Indians. The Plains Indians, which we are most concerned with here, lived on the vast, rolling, grassy plains between the Mississippi River and the Rocky Mountains. To the south, in what is now Arizona and New Mexico, were the farming Pueblo tribes, the Navaho hunters and herders and the famous Apache raiders and hunters.

The tribes of Plains Indians—among them the Blackfeet, Crow, Sioux, Cheyenne, Pawnee, Arapaho, Ute, Kiowa, Wichita and Comanche—shared many of the same characteristics. They all lived by hunting the great herds of buffalo and other game that roamed the plains. They grew to depend upon the horse after the Spanish brought it to the West, and became some of the world's most expert horsemen.

Each tribe had its important secret societies for warriors and ceremonial dances. Most of the tribes spoke dialects of the same language, but since one tribe usually could not understand the other, they developed a universal sign language. The qualities these warlike and nomadic Indians most admired were courage and endurance.

Although the Plains tribes often fought one another and raided neighboring herds of horses, they came together to fight the white buffalo hunters and settlers and the U.S. Cavalry who had been sent West to protect these intruders. The coming of the whites changed the Indians' way of life completely. The great herds of buffalo on which their existence depended were gone and their hunting grounds became ranches and farms.

It is no wonder that there was so much suspicion and so many cruel injustices between the Indian and the white man. Neither one could understand the other, and the Indian was the loser, almost obliterated by war and hatred and fear, forced at last to live on reservations.

Many movies and popular books about the Indians of the West have not been fair to them. They rarely show that the Indian had a unique civilization and was fighting to protect his territory and livelihood. Today some of the tribes are suing the U.S. Government for compensation for what was taken from them as America expanded across the plains.

The fine strong features of the typical Plains Indian and his magnificent figure, dressed in fringed buckskins and eagle feather warbonnet, mounted on a pony are familiar to everyone. Artists who lived among the Indians like George Catlin, Frederic Remington and Charles M. Russell have left stirring and realistic pictures for us, showing how the tribes lived. Today Indian artists are painting fine pictures of their ancestors' tribal life. Now you too can recapture this dramatic and picturesque era with your sketches.

Their rigorous outdoor
life helped make the In-
dians fine physical speci-
mens, capable of great
endurance.

Some typical heads of
Plains Indians.

Warbonnets

Each tribe of Indians had its own style of headdress. Feathers were added to the headdress for courageous acts in war or raids. The famous long-tailed warbonnets belonged to the most seasoned warriors.

17

The women did all the work around the camp and broke camp when it was time to travel. This left the men free to hunt and fight. The women spent most of their time making clothing and equipment.

Indian Women

Weapons

Indian weapons for both hunting and war were the bow and arrow and lance. They were used with great skill and accuracy. With the coming of the white traders, guns were substituted.

Review these simple
structural figures often.
You will soon find that no
action is too difficult to
draw.

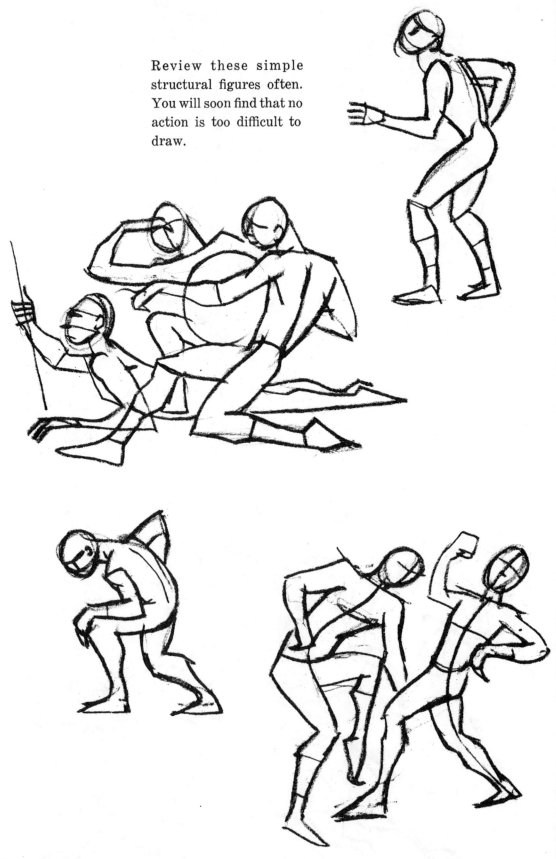

Indians ambushing an unsuspecting wagon train.

Sign Language

Indians of the Western plains used sign language to communicate with other Plains tribes and later with the white man. Some of their gestures were so expressive, no translation was needed.

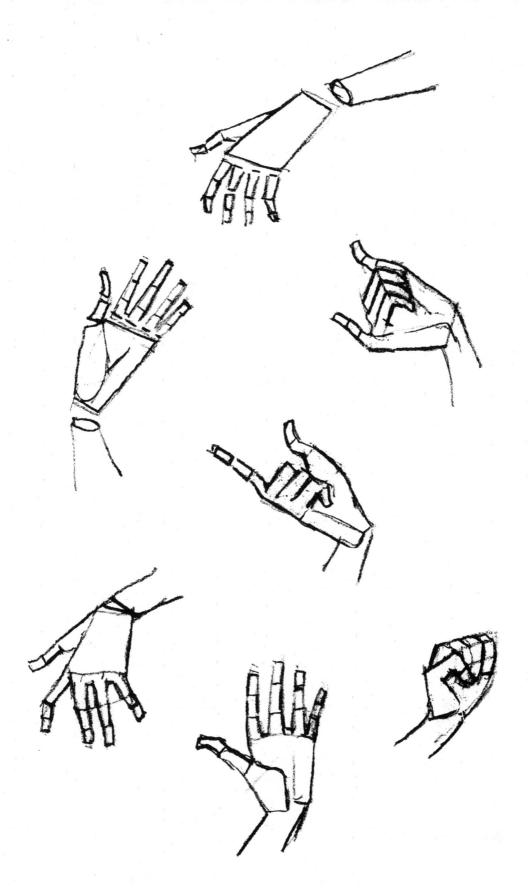

Indian Ornamentation

The Indians of the Western plains loved ornamentation and decorated themselves, their clothing, possessions and their tepees in unique ways.

They traded buffalo hides for shells, turquoise and animal claws which were supplied by tribes on the sea coasts, in the Southwest and the mountains. Later they got colorful glass beads to sew on clothing and moccasins from white traders.

Porcupine quills were dyed and embroidered in patterns on tobacco pouches, carrying cases and clothing. Feathers, fur, leather and scalps were used as fringes on shirts and leggings. Robes of buffalo hide were decorated with paintings. Unless the painting showed a battle scene or horses, their most prized possession, the Plains Indians used geometric patterns.

Warriors painted their faces and bodies with clay and plant juices in individual patterns for war parties and dances. They decorated their shields, lances, and bows and arrows. Each arrow was feathered in a pattern so a warrior could quickly claim his own. The feather warbonnets, particularly those of the Sioux and Blackfoot, were magnificent. Made of eagle feathers, they were decorated with down, quills and fur.

When you draw these handsome Indians, try to include some typical designs and decorations in your pictures to give them an authentic quality.

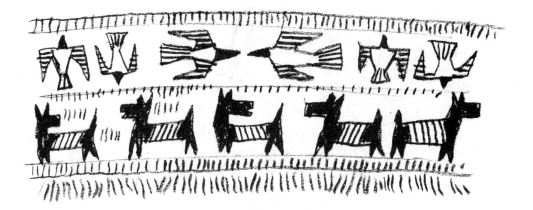

A geometrical design used to decorate clothing.

Shields were painted and often hung with eagle feathers and scalps.

Indian Dances

The dances of the Indians of the West served several purposes. Some dances were part of religious rituals. They were performed with great ceremony for hours or days at a time. They were appeals to the gods for rain, good hunting, help for the sick or for strength against their enemies. There were also dances to initiate the warriors into the secret societies of each tribe, and the famous Sun Dance and Ghost Dance, performed by most of the Plains tribes.

Other dances were in commemoration of victories or celebration of successful hunts. At these dances the Indians danced and sang and boasted of their deeds and courage.

Indian dances were highly stylized and performed with grace and rhythm. They were beautiful to watch, and many of them are still danced on reservations today.

Indian Dwellings

Most of the Plains Indians lived in skin-covered tepees which they could carry with them. Some of the early Western tribes lived in earth lodges; others at the Eastern edge of the plains built bark-covered wigwams.

In the Southwest, the Pueblo Indian tribes built "apartment houses" of adobe brick, and the Navaho herders lived in hogans of logs and earth.

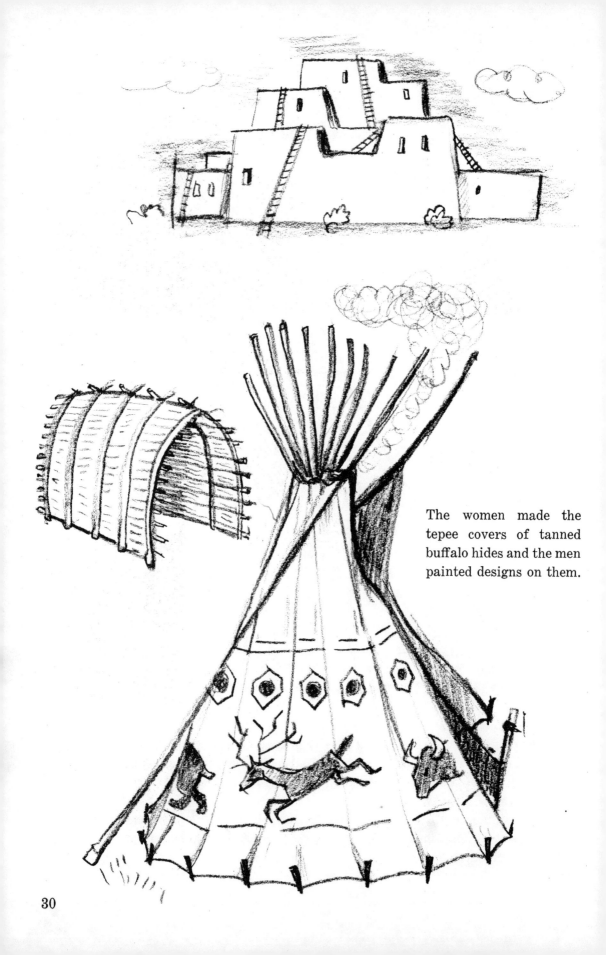

The women made the tepee covers of tanned buffalo hides and the men painted designs on them.

30

Explorers and Settlers

A Conquistador

The first explorers of the Southwest were Spanish conquistadores
who came up from Mexico. They introduced the Indians to their
first horses.   Here is a conquistador in full armor.

Mexicans settled the West long before wagon trains brought ranchers and homesteaders from the East. Aristocratic hacienda owners often owned many square miles of land, especially in Texas.

Construct your figures first as I have done here, then complete them with the necessary details.

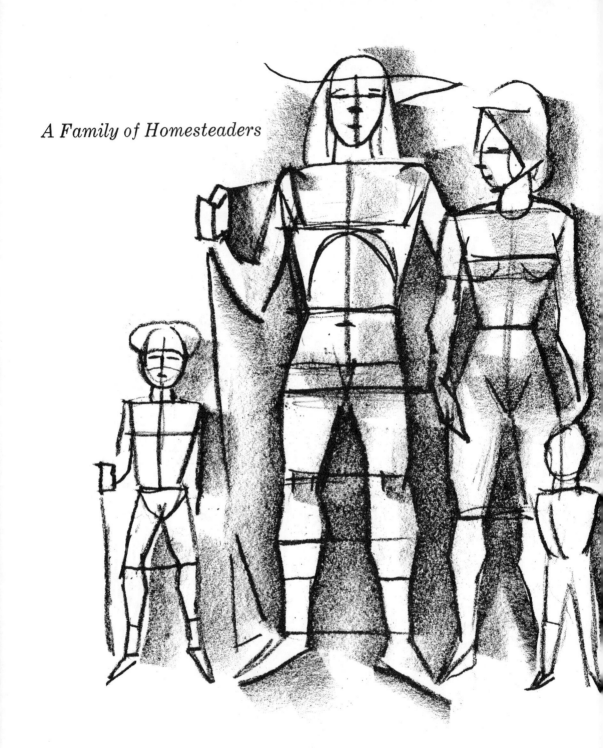

A Family of Homesteaders

Homesteaders came from the East and Midwest, looking for a new life in the West. They built log or sod huts and farmed a section of land given to them by the government.

Construct a family of homesteaders like this one, first using these simple geometric forms. Then put in details similar to those on the next page.

A Mexican Peon Family

A great part of the American Southwest and Texas used to belong to
Mexico and was settled by Mexicans.

Mexican peasants or *peons* worked on the large haciendas, farming
or ranching.

Sketch a rough outline of the people first, then fill in the details.

Cowboys

The first cattle were brought to America by the Spanish conquistadores and from them grew the great herds of longhorns which grazed on the limitless plains of the West. These herds of cattle needed herdsmen. The hard-riding, sun-wind- and rain-hardened men who tended the herds came to be called cowboys.

Everyone in America learns in childhood about a cowboy's life on the range. It was a hard life but a free one, full of range riding, fighting rustlers, bronco busting, roundups and branding and long, dangerous trail drives to bring the cattle to the railroad and market.

Books and movies have made us familiar with all the daily chores of the cowboy. Children still play games of cowboys and Indians, using six-shooters and lariats and wearing chaps, boots and ten gallon hats.

What theme could therefore be more suitable as a subject for your drawings than the life of the cowboy? This wealth of material on the cowboy is already in your head, material that is both romantic and exciting.

Let your memory of what you've seen and read and your imagination play with scenes of cowboy life on your drawing paper.

Try to be authentic when drawing the cowboy's clothing and equipment and the action of men and animals as well as the Western background.

Use some of the details shown in these pages, then tap other sources for scenes of cowboy life. Best of all give full range to your memory and imagination. Draw simply but with care.

Bulldogging

The Cowboy's Daily Chores

Branding

ROUNDUP TIME

Bulldogging and branding make fine themes for action drawings.

Roping

Roping steers and horses calls for skillful work with a lariat and is beautiful to watch and draw.

Lariats

The word lariat comes from the Spanish word *reata*, the braided rawhide rope used by the Mexican cowboys or *vaqueros*. A lariat is also known as a lasso, and can be made of hemp. No cowboy was without a lasso and often could do fancy tricks with it.

Bucking Broncos

In rodeos a bronc rider is allowed only one rein to control the bucking horse. He can also hold on to or touch the horse or saddle with only one hand.

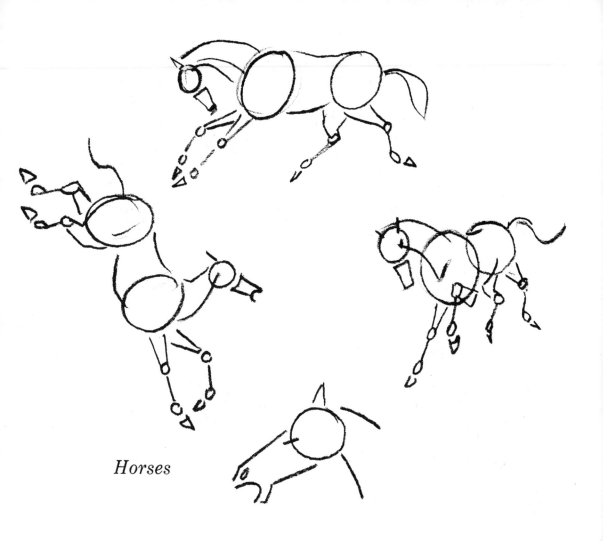

Horses

Practice drawing these simple diagrams of horses in action. They
will be the basis for your finished drawings.

Here are the horses of the previous page saddled and mounted by
their cowboy riders. Notice how little detail was required to make the
basic horse forms come alive.

The Cowboy's Equipment

Decorative tooled leather saddle A cowboy's saddle was one of his most prized possessions.

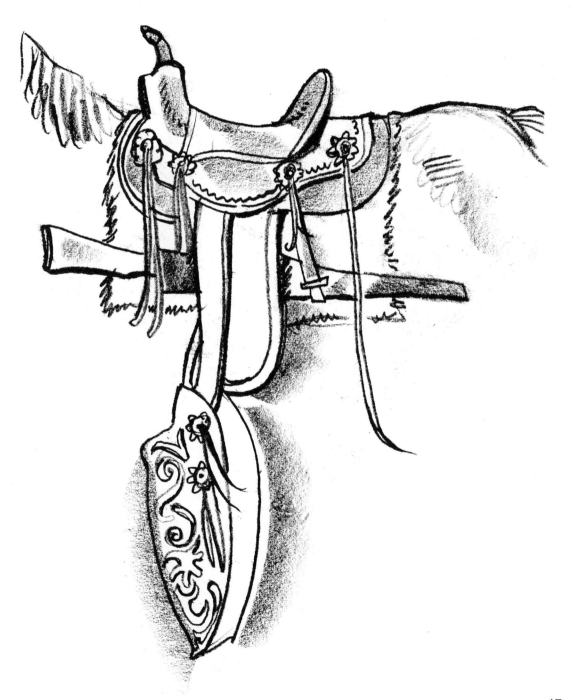

Chaps, Sombreros and Boots

The clothing worn by cowboys was both distinctive and practical.

Chaps, an abbreviation of the Mexican word *chaparreras,* were leather or hide leg coverings worn by *vaqueros* and cowboys for protection in sagebrush country.

Sombreros, also known as ten-gallon hats, were very necessary in the hot Western sun. Mexican sombreros had a wider brim and higher peak than those favored by the American cowboy.

Western boots were always made with high heels, and often were decorated with fancy tooling and stitching.

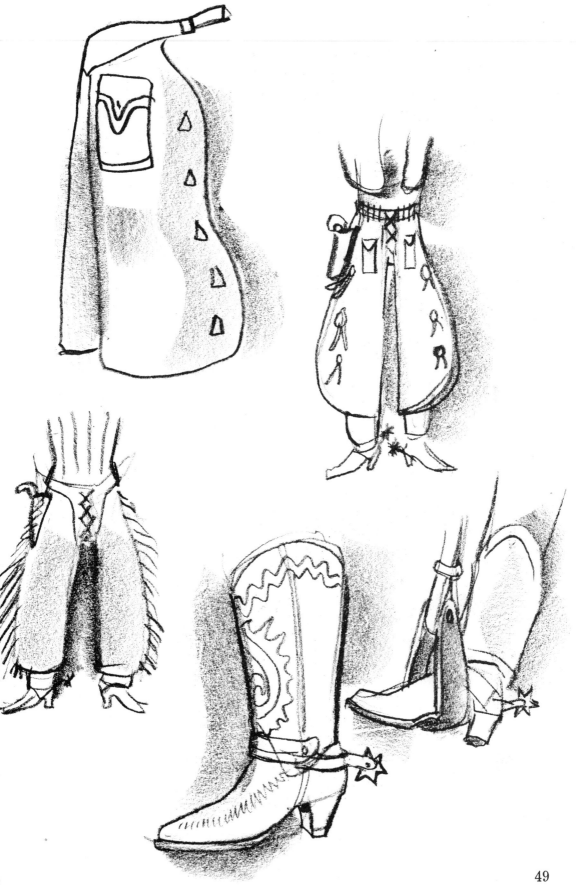

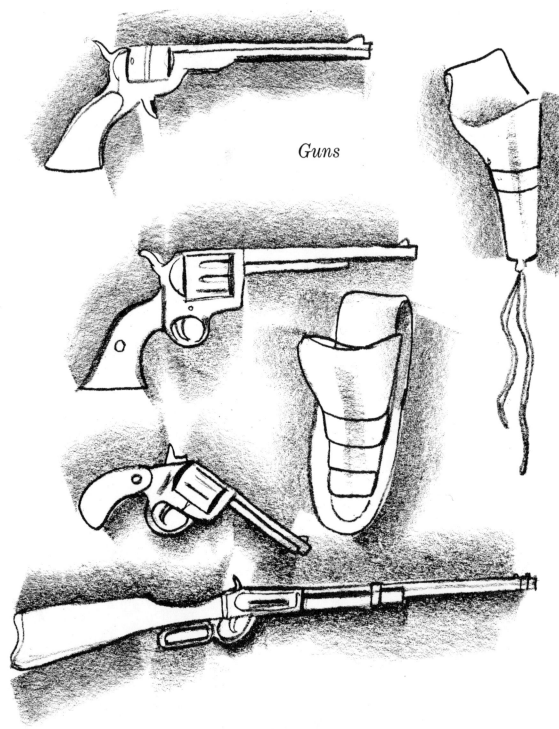

Guns

The Colt six-shooter and the Remington and Winchester rifles were the basic weapons of the old West against wild animals and rustlers and marauding Indians.

The leather thongs dangling from one of the holsters were used to tie it to the cowhand's leg so that he could draw quickly.

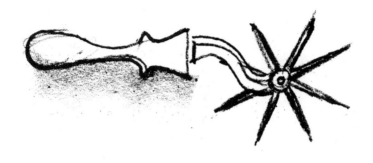

Spurs

Spurs of Western cowhands differed considerably.

The California cowboys, influenced by the Mexican *vaqueros,* used spurs with long, sharp rowels. The protruding spikes of the rowels turned like the spokes of a wheel.

Texans wore spurs with less protruding spikes.

Some spurs were designed to make a musical jingle-jangle when the cowboy walked.

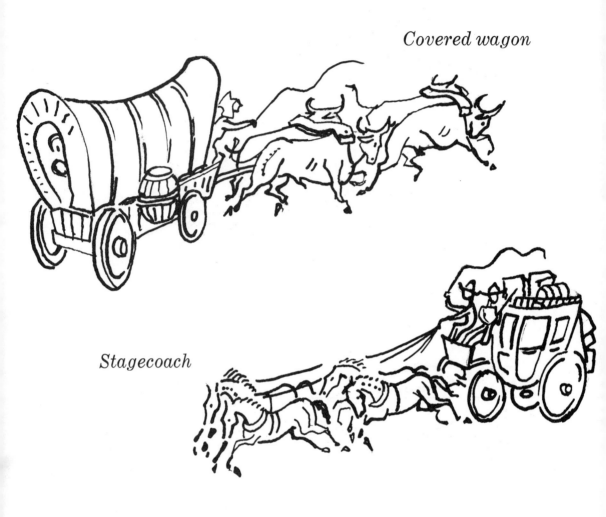

Covered wagon

Stagecoach

Traveling and Living in the West

BEFORE THE RAILROADS

Before the railroads came to the West, these were the three major means of transport for people and their belongings.

The stagecoach carried passengers, mail and payrolls.

The covered wagon, drawn by oxen, brought settlers and homesteaders from the East. Wagons banded together in long trains for protection from the Indians.

Indians invented the travois, an A-shaped frame of tepee poles dragged by a horse or a dog, to carry their possessions.

Travois

Covered wagon

Stagecoach

Railroads

The railroads began to extend their tracks across the West soon after the Civil War. This meant that cattlemen no longer had to drive their herds hundreds of miles to sell them. The exciting and dangerous days of the trail drive were over for the cowboy.

The railroads also made it easier for settlers to reach the West, and towns were established. The cowboy added fence riding to his chores as the open range was broken up by homesteaders.

Here is an example of the "Iron Horse" which changed the character of the Wild West.

Buildings and Towns

Houses were small and built of logs until sawmills made clapboard available.

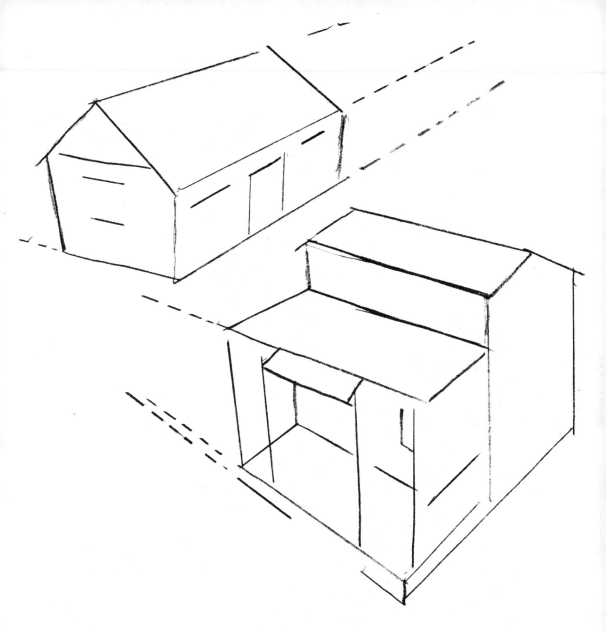

Using these perspective sketches as a guide, draw a typical main street of a Western cow town.

Fill in details from your memory of Western towns in the movies.

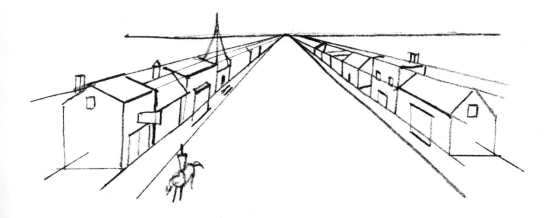

Light-weight, birch-bark canoes were another means of swift transportation used by the Indians.

Prospectors

Prospectors roamed all over the West looking for gold and silver, accompanied only by their burros.

Animals of the Wild West

This book does not attempt to deal in detail with all of the many animals of the West. Other books in this series have shown a number of animals both wild and domesticated that are associated with the West. Your drawings of Western animals should include wolves, pumas, coyotes and many rodents and snakes as well as cattle, horses and sheep.

However the buffalo, the longhorn and Indian pony and the horse of the cowboy are so important in depicting the West that steps in drawing them are repeated in this section and throughout the book.

Notice that the essential structure of these animals may be expressed in very simple terms. Study their gait, running, walking and grazing.

Do not try to make "finished," detailed drawings of these animals, or for that matter, of any of the characters and scenes of the Wild West.

Try to express in the most simple fashion possible the basic character of the animals. Use the most direct action to give your impression of their story.

You will find that in eliminating everything but essential actions and anatomy, your animals will "live." Pictures you draw of them will be visual, exciting stories of how you feel about the Wild West.

Burros and Mules

The Mexican burro and the American mule were often used to haul freight. Drawing them in their many moods is great fun.

Buffalos

Study these buffalos which have been reduced to simple geometric forms, then draw them.

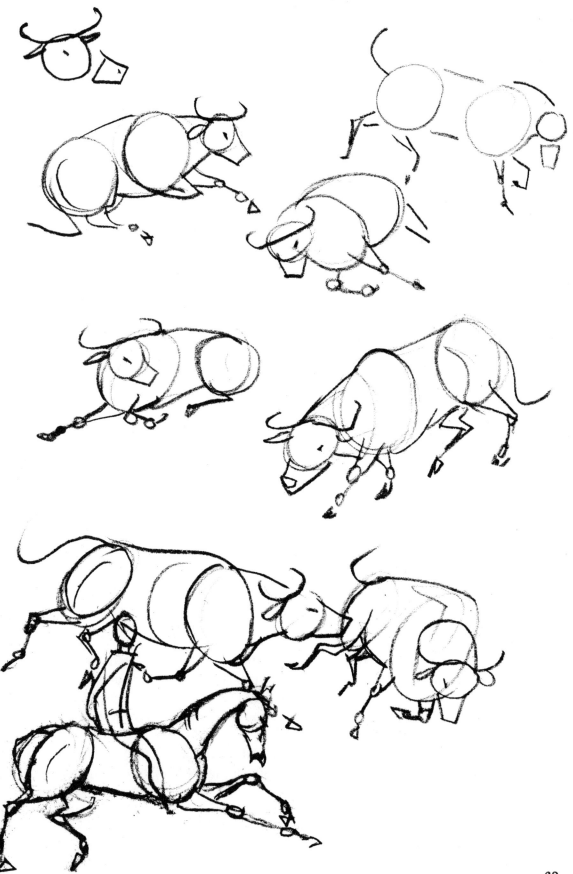

63

Final Word

You have traveled the Wild West with me in these pages but you have seen it through my eyes, not your own. Now try to visualize your own West and what it means to you. Say what you want to say about it with as much honesty and excitement as you can.

The most important quality you have as an artist is your own individual response to what you see. Your responses are sharpened by your own tastes and emotions and by your special "handwriting," or style of drawing, in putting what you see on paper.

Be as authentic as you can in your drawings, but do not sacrifice spontaneity for authenticity. If you do that, after acquiring some knowledge of proportion and form, your drawings should be good. With practice and talent you eventually may even produce fine pictures.

Above all, have fun when you draw. You will find that your own pleasure in your work will give pleasure to others when they look at your pictures.